Irene Smith believes we can use all our senses given to us by God to help others in today's world. She enjoys painting, stained-glass making, flower arranging, garden planning as well as writing.

Having previously lived in Wales, she gained an MA. Theol. from St. Andrews University, St Andrews, Scotland and then studied at the Nazarene College, Manchester, England for an MA module in Spirituality. She has continued her studies by reading about religions, cultures, and spirituality.

While her MS symptoms were being managed in hospital, she found every time that encounters and conversations with others made a difference to her life and of those she met.

To my dad (departed)

And to his grandson

Philip Jason, my son

Irene Smith

DIVINE MYSTIQUE II

Divine God Mystique Awe

AUSTIN MACAULEY PUBLISHERS™
LONDON * CAMBRIDGE * NEW YORK * SHARJAH

Copyright © Irene Smith 2024

The right of Irene Smith to be identified as author of this work has been asserted by the author in accordance with sections 77 and 78 of the Copyright, Designs and Patents Act 1988.

All rights reserved. No part of this publication may be reproduced, stored in a retrieval system or transmitted in any form or by any means, electronic, mechanical, photocopying, recording or otherwise, without the prior permission of the publishers.

Any person who commits any unauthorised act in relation to this publication may be liable to criminal prosecution and civil claims for damages.

A CIP catalogue record for this title is available from the British Library.

ISBN 9781035839384 (Paperback)
ISBN 9781035839391 (Hardback)
ISBN 9781035839407 (ePub e-book)

www.austinmacauley.com

First Published 2024
Austin Macauley Publishers Ltd®
1 Canada Square
Canary Wharf
London
E14 5AA

Acknowledgments

I wish to thank a lovely friend, Jill, and acknowledge her hard work in typing all the manuscript – which I cannot manage because of a medical condition – but also the support she has given me throughout the writing of this manuscript. She has also kept an eye on my spelling and punctuation, and for explaining a "split infinitive", that needed correction!

I would also like to thank my carer and friend, Shapna, whose help and support I have appreciated too.

Stained Glass by Ian Reynolds

Creation Portrayed in Stained-Glass.
Together with the Kingdom of Heaven

Creation – the landscape in right hand corner, sweeps up to and across the Kingdom of Heaven. This effect is shown by small textured, coloured pieces of stained glass. All pieces are collected and placed together then leaded, as the representation of creation. Leaded lines sweep from God's creation up to the Kingdom of Heaven. Naturally, the Kingdom of Heaven is larger – shown by the area deepened and rising. We don't know of any further life living outside our universe and part of God's Kingdom. Scientists work hard in this decade as do theologians, academics, philosophers etc. to find and link together all knowledge.

Representative in this stained-glass piece of work are silvery birds swirling around in a current of air and up into the heavens. Maybe they foretell of angels in the Kingdom of Heaven? Looking at the glints of gold pieces of glass in the upper area of the work and textures, might we discern with further study, other dimensions or ideas.

Table of Contents

Preface	13
Nature's Spring Unfolds	14
Spring Music	16
God's Wonder	18
Springtime with the Easter Passion	19
Palm Sunday	20
A Hymn	21
Meek and Mild	22
Triduum	23
Maundy Thursday	24
The Verdict of Jesus	26
The Events of Good Friday	27
The Burial of Jesus	30
The Easter Passion in History	32
Easter Sunday	33
In Conclusion Final Thoughts	35
I Design and Make	37
Summertime	39
Summer	41
The Christian Endeavour Leads Onwards	42
The Large and Small	43
The Frozen Lake	45

Memory Time	47
Girl in the Photograph	49
Ukraine	52
Empathy	54
The Question	55
Faith in Action	56
Autumn Meditation	57
Christmas and Later	59
Have You Lost Something?	60
The Jewel of Christmas	61
Angel of Hope	62
The Nativity	63
Zechariah and the Meeting of the Two Cousins	66
John the Baptist	68
Mary and Joseph	70
Mary and Joseph Journey to Bethlehem	71
At the Stable	72
News for the Shepherds	75
Final Thoughts	78
The Circle of Love	80
Eternity Is Timeless	81
Bibliography	82

Preface

This second book of mine, *Divine Mystique II,* begins with two birds which were featured in book one – the Blackbird and Robin Redbreast. They've popped up here to say, "Hello" again.

This book combines stories and poems with accounts of the Nativity and the Easter Passion with Bible references. Written in a format of prose and poetry with illustrations between several of the pages, these paintings act as a further voice in explanations to help readers understand the meaning of faith in Christianity.
Irene Smith

Nature's Spring Unfolds

The pansies smile up at Christ,
The tulips bow down to God.
Cascading pink blossom flies overall,
And settles in fancy piles for
The children to play with.
Our beloved blackbird watches.

Tiny buds and leaves are joyously,
Showing a welcome, to the trinity.
Whispering sounds of praise run
Through grasses tall, and show the
Mesmerising, beautiful, green shades, one
Associates with an English spring.

The first red rose looking to summer,
Glows with pride, and opens its petals
To send out love and fragrance to all.
The surrounding buds stand proudly
Round the opened rose, whilst looking
On is our beloved blackbird.

Oops! I nearly forgot!
The daisies, dandelions and
Buttercups, wish to join in
Praising our Lord, too.
Tall and elegant, small and sweet.
Humans and plants alike, praise Christ.

Spring Music

It's here again, springtime joy
    It's here again, in glorious melody.
    Colours rise to tips of musical notes.
    A shower of stars swirls in tune
    And hover over signs of nature's re-birth
    Joy to the world, we sing. (Hymn)

The lovely pink, small tulips,
    Open their double petals to
    Worship God; beside the pink
    Magnolia tree, opening early to
    Join in the worship to God.
    Green leaved ferns start unfurling
    Their stems, to greet the spring
    Sunshine…and Christ.

Tiny leaves and buds are happily
    Showing welcome to the Trinity.
    Colours from nature, and some
    Manufactured by garden lovers; add
    A musical chorus of flowers.
    The famous "Chelsea Flower Show"
    In London, at this time of year, brings
    Forth wondrous displays of floral art.
    Also, how to use nature's gifts for our
    Health and well-being.

Around the central mass of blooms,
    And those intertwined between new
    Shoots and up trees, the vertical climb
Can be seen from clematis flowers in a range
    Of colours. This can remind us of music
    Reaching a crescendo, the musical notes
    And flowers pointing up to the Heavens.
    Bluebells' tiny flower heads, ring
    Out like bells imitating quaver notes
    On musical scores. We listen to church
Bells ringing out to us "Come" to services,
    Where we sing and praise God,
    From our hearts. Alleluia.

God's Wonder

A first sunrise lit the
Earth as God called light, for
His creation of our world.
As darkness fell away, the first
Sunrise shone forth with little
Drops of sunlight falling onto
The cold, hard earth below.

A chorus of birdsong rings
Out, just before the last threads
Of darkness, fade into obscurity.
The birdsong sounds like
Trumpeters heralding a special moment.
It brings us *Joy* and a new
Day is ushered in by our
Dawn chorus.
A gift from God.

Springtime with the Easter Passion

At springtime, bulbs and seeds grow and flourish much to our delight. The mornings and evenings become lighter too. Joy is felt when we see our gardens and free open spaces begin to fill with colour, even the smallest of window boxes. When trees begin to blossom, followed by green buds and leaves, hope rises for new life. But these moments can be tainted by Satan's presence. Don't let him destroy the joy and hope of the new season. Strengthen your resolve to resist temptation. God's Holy Spirit is here to help you so just ask/pray to Him to help you.

During spring, we recall our memories and bring forth the history of our religion. This is often taught in schools and churches and re-enacted in small groups; followed by music, films, and plays, of the Eastertime Passion. From our Holy Bible, the scripts are drawn, and artwork inspired from young to older artists. The sign of Christianity ☙ was often found in the catacombs of ancient Rome, where the very early Christians hid, and lived, from the Roman aggressors. Any Christians who were caught faced gruesome deaths, by being fed to the lions, where an excited audience revelled in the so-called show. In AD 70, the emperor Constantine converted to Christianity and his subjects followed his religion as ordered (on the surface).

Palm Sunday

A week before the actual crucifixion, on the Sunday we name as Palm Sunday, we find Jesus going to Jerusalem. He asked two of his disciples to go and find the colt tied up and waiting for them. A colt is the offspring of an ass. These two disciples went and found the colt as Jesus had directed. Someone put a cloak over the colt's back and Jesus mounted upon him. Then an excited crowd spread palm leaves aloft in a frenzy of misplaced excitement. The crowds thought that when Jesus reached the temple in Jerusalem, he was going to declare himself the long-awaited Messiah/King, who would also deal with the hated Romans. But Jesus was not in war apparel and meekly arrived in Jerusalem, sitting on a young colt. Many of the crowd were puzzled and disappointed.

I enclose here a poem from G.K. Chesterton that seems appropriate to use as a prayer on Palm Sunday. Jesus was arriving at Jerusalem to bring forth a new Kingdom for the crowds. But not one of violence, gained by force, but the "Kingdom of God", bringing us salvation, forgiveness and love. Although we now know and welcome the Kingdom of Heaven and God's Holy Spirit, there were not many people at that time that had come to faith and believed in the new creation that Christ formed on the cross.

A Hymn

O God of earth and altar,
Bow down and hear our cry,
Our earthly rulers falter,
Our people drift and die;
The walls of gold entomb us,
The swords of scorn divide,
Take not thy thunder from us,
But take away our pride.

G. K. Chesterton

And to end this section of Palm Sunday at the beginning of Holy Week, we read these few lines:-

Meek and Mild

By Janet Greenland

Blessed are the meek,
For they shall inherit the earth.
Behold, thy King cometh unto thee,
Meek, and sitting upon an ass colt.

The Holy Week and events, and trials for Jesus, had begun.

Triduum

Towards the end of Holy Week, we enter the TRIDUUM. This is three days – Maundy Thursday – Good Friday and Holy Saturday, that merge into one long day, for the Christian Church. This longest day is comprised of late evening on the Thursday – to early morning Easter Sunday. The meaning of TRIDUUM is a religious observance lasting three days.

In John's gospel in the New Testament of the Bible, Jesus was having supper with his disciples, which turned out to be the "Last Supper", (as we now know it.) During this time, Jesus says to Judas, (Iscariot) 'Do quickly what you are going to do,' and Judas leaves the table abruptly. Unbeknown to the other disciples this was the first move towards Judas betraying his master, to the Roman and temple officials, for a purse of silver (money). Jesus knew it was the first step of God's heavenly plan, to redeem and save his sinning children throughout the ages.

Before they left the table of Jesus told his disciples that he was giving them a New Commandment:

"__Love one another as I have loved you.__"

Maundy Thursday

After the Last Supper, Jesus rose with his disciples and went to the Garden of Gethsemane) or Mount of Olives). He asked his disciples to wait and watch out for him. He went to pray to his Father in a secluded place. His prayers were agonised and distressed. He asked his Father to take away the bitter scenario before him – he said, 'But not my will, Father, but yours.' An angel came down from heaven to give him strength. This was the last time we see or hear angels, until after his crucifixion. This last journey, Jesus must do on his own.

Upon returning to his disciples, Jesus found them sleeping. Suddenly, Jesus found himself confronted by the Roman soldiers who had come to arrest him. The disciples woke up, scared and confused at the sight of the soldiers. Peter tried violence and cut off the ear of a servant who was in the party to arrest Jesus. The ear was quickly healed by Jesus who said, 'He came not to do violence.' Next, Judas Iscariot stepped forward and betrayed his master with a kiss. After this sign, the soldiers led Jesus away to the temple. All the disciples fled in fear. But Peter hung around, in a courtyard, to hear and see what was happening. He did not realise that here he would deny Jesus three times, when the cock crowed, early morning. As soon as he heard the cock crow, he realised, for Jesus had told him earlier and Peter had protested that this would never happen.

So, the soldiers and the Jewish police had arrested Jesus, bound him and took him to a temple official, Annas, then Caiaphas, the High Priest. Jesus was struck in the face by a Jewish policeman. This was the first blow of the tortuous night to follow. He was taken to Pontius Pilate, the governor, representing the Roman emperor. Finding nothing to convict Jesus of Pilate handed him back. Jesus was spat upon, mocked by the soldiers, and dressed in a purple robe (the colour of kings). They placed a crown of thorns upon his head and took him back to Pontius Pilate.

Crowds had massed in and around the temple and Pilate brought out Jesus to stand in front of them. He told the crowds he found nothing to convict him of and Jesus could be freed. But the crowd kept shouting, 'Crucify him! Crucify him!' All the Pharisees and the temple officials joined in with the crowd's cries. These crowds did not include those from Palm Sunday's triumphant procession leading towards Jerusalem. Most of those crowds were innocent of the politics and issues going on in the Temple, against Jesus. Their celebration journey was to take Jesus to the Temple there, so he could declare himself as the Messiah who had come to declare himself as their King and overthrow the hated Romans. They lacked the understanding of the Kingdom of Heaven and Jesus Christ who was the Son of God, leading them to eternity.

The Verdict of Jesus

The crowds continued screaming, 'Crucify him!' to Pontius Pilate. The Jewish Passover was taking place, a very important feast and time for them (as it is now). It was a custom that Pilate, as the Roman Governor, had to uphold. Having three robbers due for crucifixion that the crowd could free one of the robbers at this time. So, when again Pilate asked them to free Jesus – the crowd screamed, 'Barabbas!' Pilate asked for some water, and washed his hands in resignation, in front of the crowds. This was his sign that the outcome of the verdict was nothing to do with himself. He put himself clear of all responsibility. The verdict on Jesus of Nazareth was *crucifixion*. Pilate ordered Jesus to be flogged and taken away.

The Events of Good Friday

Early morning, the condemned criminals were set upon the road to Golgotha (or the Place of the Skull.) Each criminal had to carry their own heavy wooden cross, on which they would be crucified. It was a tormented agonising journey. The last journey that Jesus of Nazareth, in a totally human body, would take on earth.

When reaching Golgotha, the wooden crosses were flung on the ground, with the rusty nails, then the prisoners stripped of their garments, for the soldiers to lay bets for. Then the crucifixions began. When Jesus was stretched over the cross and nailed to it, his suffering was to a degree we will never comprehend. The crosses were raised, with Jesus's bearing the sign "King of the Jews" over his head.

The other two crosses each side of Jesus held two men who exchanged words between themselves and Jesus. They did not seem like robbers or criminals, as the gospels seem to indicate, but more like political rebels or taunting failed idealists. They had wanted a better land or country and used violence or inducements of it, against the Roman power now I force under Pontius Pilate, who was answerable to Caesar himself. But the Romans did not understand about the other kingdom that was talked about, the Kingdom of Heaven, and so wanted to have these three men insurrectionists, troublemakers – out of the way before the Jewish Passover feast. *Hence, the crucifixion took place quickly.*

The first criminal spoke to Jesus, with that saying, 'Can't you help yourself and us as you are supposed to be the Messiah?'

Then the other criminal rebuked him and replied, 'We are receiving the punishments we deserved, but this person called Jesus has not done anything wrong.' Surprisingly, he showed a degree of faith and turned his head towards Jesus. He continued to say, 'Jesus, remember me when you come into your kingdom.' A reference to this passage in Luke's gospel (Luke 23: 39–43).

In reply, Jesus said, 'Truly, this day you will be with me in Paradise.'

Paradise is a term used for the Kingdom of Heaven. Here we find the Divine Garden created by God. We sometimes hear of it called the Garden of Eden. But the Garden was defiled by Adam and Eve, the first humans that God formed. They were given, by God, the whole garden to live in, but with one proviso – *they were not to touch any fruit from the tree of life in the centre of the garden.* Here the first *sin* in the first creation occurred. Eve was tempted by the serpent (the Satan) who was in the tree, to take and taste some of its fruit.

She took the apple for Adam to taste, which he did. Then he realised it was the fruit of the tree of life. That evening, as God was walking in the garden, Adam and Eve hid themselves behind bushes because they realised that they were naked. They had not realised this fact before they ate the fruit from the forbidden tree. Plus, they felt guilty because they had broken God's proviso. This deed had made negative feelings and disobedience enter creation – the first sin. So, Adam and Eve learnt that consequences must be faced for their actions.

Jesus Speaks on the Cross and brings the New Creation into being.

After the brief exchange with the two men either side of him, Jesus begins to speak. He spoke his most creative work in his time on earth. He spoke just seven words, each one outlining a section and meaning for the New Creation, coming into being after his death. This New Creation would lead us to the Kingdom of Heaven, to be with us *now*.

The original creation, "spoken into being" by God, had been abused and broken and continually sinned against. Here from the cross, speaking the New Creation into being for all, Jesus was aware of his impending death.

But before we go any further from the cross, perhaps we should read about the words Jesus spoke before his death and burial. Looking down from the cross, Jesus saw his mother and a much-loved disciple standing at the foot of the cross. He said to his mother, 'Woman, here is your son.' Then he said to his disciple, 'Here is your mother.' From then on, the disciple took Mary into his own house and cared for her. (John 19: 26–27)

About noon, the whole land became dark. Jesus gave a loud cry, 'My God, my God, why have you forsaken me?' In response, someone offered to Jesus a stick that had a sponge on the end containing sour wine, for him to drink. After taking a mouthful, Jesus cried out again. *'Father, into your hands I commend my Spirit.'*

Then he bowed his head. It was over. It was about 3.00 in the afternoon. The temple curtain split from one end to the other, signifying that the old way of worshipping was over.

The Sabbath rest began.

As God had decreed for himself and everyone, after he had formed the first creation, so Jesus did the same after he spoke the second creation into being. After his death, Jesus entered the Sabbath rest. The Sabbath was/is on a Saturday for the Jewish race. Jesus was born a Jew. For three days, we presume that Jesus lay in his tomb to rise on the third day, Easter Sunday.

The Burial of Jesus

Joseph and Nicodemus, towards evening, asked Pontius Pilate if they could have Jesus's body to bury. Agreement was given (for all bodies had to be taken down from their crosses before the Jewish Sabbath the next day – Holy Saturday.)

Imagine these two men, one very old, doing this very gruesome task. They may have had servants which they could supervise, but it would not have lessened their grief. They took Jesus's body to a new tomb which had been prepared for Joseph himself. The two old secretive disciples took this task themselves as the other disciples had fled in fear. As for Judas, we will hear about him a little later. Secrecy of their discipleship did not seem to matter anymore to Joseph and very old Nicodemus – both believed in Jesus and his message.

Jesus was laid out in the tomb and his body anointed with oils then bound with white cloths. One cloth was laid over his face. That was the custom in those times. Next a large white boulder sealed the entrance to the tomb.

A note of interest here:

The oils brought by Nicodemus to anoint Jesus's body, were a costly amount. This reminds us of the *Three Wise Men* from the East, who saw the "new star" shining brightly and set out to find the new baby – the Holy baby. Their gifts of gold, *frankincense and myrrh* were significant when linked to the holy babe, born a stable, whose life was ended by crucifixion, at Golgotha, on a rough wooden cross.

Did the *three Wise Men* years after, realise how their gifts were used; and how they impacted in world history?

I mentioned earlier that we could return to Judas Iscariot and see how he fared. "The Ballad of the Judas Tree" by Ruth Etchells (1931–2012) tells of God's forgiveness. I hope some of you might have heard it previously. It is often used in churches at Easter-time especially in Scotland.

Ruth Etchells 1931–2012 was one of the most influential women in the Church of England, a university lecturer and poet. She had a rare compassion, intensity and visionary quality balanced by a self-deprecating wit. And a depth of intuition which made her a good spiritual director and chaplain.

(From the obituary in "The Guardian" dated 27 August 2012, and from the Church of Scotland website for Easter day 2022.)

The Easter Passion in History

With sustained human effort
We serve our Holy Father
Through his son,
Jesus Christ our Lord,
Who ascended into heaven
From the **Cross.**

In his wake, the
Clouds billowed out
With rapturous, golden
Swirls, from the wise Men
In the East, who had
Followed our Saviour
From his human birth,
Under the shining **Star**.

Our holy Saviour
Brought together the
Old and the New creation,
To fulfil God's New covenant.
And bring the Kingdom-of-Heaven
To be with us **Now.**
Alleluia

Easter Sunday

Very early on the third day of Jesus's entombment, Mary Magdalene, with some other women disciples, approached the tomb. They had come to attend to the aftercare of the body of Jesus, as was the custom in those days. For Mary Magdalene, it was the continuing of her love and respect for her master/teacher. Drawing near, they were aghast to see the huge boulder that sealed the tomb entrance had been rolled away.

Mary Magdalene peered in and saw two figures dressed in white at each end of where Jesus's body should have been lain. Here the angels reappear. Though her tears and bewilderment and grief Mary Magdalene asked where the body of her Lord was. The angle told her he had risen, and he repeated this to her firmly. Mary turned as she sensed a figure behind her. The figure said, 'Mary.'

She recognised Jesus immediately replying, 'Rabbani,' meaning Teacher. Mary Magdalene tried to touch him, but Jesus said no – he had not risen to his Holy Father yet. Then the women rushed off to tell the other disciples the glorious news. This was the first appearance of the Risen Jesus Christ, before he returned to his father.

(*Note 1 – Jesus' first risen appearance was to the* women *disciples.*)

(Note 2 – There is a second account from the New Testament writing that is about Mary Magdalene, when she discovers her Lord's body is not in the tomb. She sees a figure in white whom she takes to be a gardener and asks him if he knows where her Lord's body has been taken. When the figure says her name, Mary instantly recognises Jesus. Reaching out to touch him, as in Note 1's account, Jesus says, no he has not risen to his Holy Father yet.)

Many women disciples who helped Jesus during his ministry are rarely spoken of in the gospels. But today we are led by female ministers (priests) in church, as well as chaplains in hospitals and prisons, simply, wherever they are needed.

Many female theologians have written copious books on elements of the Christian faith and problems throughout the ages, including now, in our times.

Moral thoughts and physical reality link up to form the modern disciple.

There is suffering in these contemporary times as there was in Jesus's time on earth, and after his crucifixion. Signs and symbols were found scratched or painted on the rocky walls of the catacombs on the outskirts of Ancient Rome. This was where the early Christians fled to hide – or live – when pursued by the Roman soldiers under the orders of Pontius Pilate or Caesar, When, or if, they were caught, they suffered horrendous deaths. Many books by scholars have been written about this era and relay specific details to students who are on degree courses to study the life of Our Lord Jesus Christ.

Jesus Christ on the cross worked and suffered to save God's creation and bring us salvation and forgiveness. He brought Heaven down to us and a new way of worshipping was put into place.

If we reach out to God in despair, Christ brings us hope and love from his Father. If we struggle to find our lost way through troubled times, the light of Christ will shine before us and lead onwards to a pathway of strength and purpose. Whether we, or I personally, worship in private, in a house group, or in a church congregation, I feel joy at receiving God's love and grace into my life. I sincerely hope you do also.

In Conclusion
Final Thoughts

I wonder if I have extended, just a little, your knowledge and faith of God and his love for us. May we all listen for God's Holy Spirit to lead us, as we worship and pray with love, to our Heavenly Father through Jesus Christ, his Son.

If you have any questions, I have no answers for you. Your own answers must come from communion between you and God.

May I ask you – what it is you want from your Christian faith? Or how would you thank God? He has his own way of meeting you in Faith and Love.

"Lord, abide with us."

May you find inner PEACE.
Irene

Thoughts and Reflections For Your Interest

I Design and Make

I design and make
Changes, and learn of
New plants to grow, through
The changing seasons.
As I opened my door
And looked out at
My garden,
God's love wrapped
Around me, and warmth
And happiness,
Filled my being.

I do what I can
With help from my
Gardener, to keep the
Garden as lovely as
I can, for my Lord.
I may end in pain,
I may have to shuffle
Around, as my mobility
Deserts me. My painful
Hands (from carpal tunnel syndrome)
Keep dropping things.
But my heart is full
Of love for my Lord.

I work to offer God
A garden of peace and love.
One where I go to
Pray and meet Him.
I take tears sometimes,
But laughter and joy too,
my smile is wide as
I look to the sky
And see a backdrop,
Of beautiful blue

Holding up fluffy clouds
With shining edges.
A silver lining some say.
So, as I venture out
Into my garden, I have
Prayers and praise ready
For you Lord, God. Gloria.
May your Holy Grace and love
Spread outwards from the
Garden, to others that enjoy it.
May my happy Blackbird
Join in by whistling his
Praise, also.
To my Holy Father, Alleluia.
"Alleluia"

Summertime

A shaft of sunlight
Burst through grey and
Dismal clouds. The outcome
Of a dull and morose life.
The sunlight lit up and
Dazzled the eyes, then revealed
A pathway leading to God's
Call to you and us.

Pick from the basket of
Fish that is offered.
Nourishment to appease
Your hunger and emptiness.
Follow God's call along
The pathway of life; led
By Christ's church and
The Holy Spirit.

As you journey, pick up
And scatter the seeds
Of knowledge and love.
Absorb these then
Stretch out for more.
For you are the pupil
And teacher in one. Hold
Out your hands – and lead.

Summer

Some sunny spells
Some blustery times
Some sunny aspects
Loading pools of gold.
These parts metaphorically
Take the form of clarity
Within our thought.
Shining rays lead
Onto peaceful paths, lit
By our Saviour's eternal light.
This heavenly light
Transforms our lives,
As we follow it to
God's kingdom of love,
So let the golden pools
Spread their mystique,
Into and around, our
Wondering minds.
And let us listen for
The still, small voice
Of God.

The Christian Endeavour Leads Onwards

The Christian endeavour leads onwards
Hopefully to gain eternity's peace,
When time and age become one.

The incandescent rays of life-light show
Actions focussed with mercenary intent,
Differing in evil destruction of man and earth.

Thus, causing homelessness, starvation,
Poverty, and illness
With no safety for babies or infants.
No comfort for grief stricken or injured victims.

Timeframes continue before Christ with Roman and Jewish slaughter alike.
followed by racial and genocidal hate
Throughout the ages and religious extremism.

Ignored is the Divine Law of creation for man and creature.
Creation given to man by God
To use and maintain for the good of all.

To live in harmony and peace is the new hope for man.
A doubtful hope – maybe
But the Christian endeavour leads onwards.
"God made us to be His children. Let us WORSHIP and PRAISE Him, Through Jesus Christ our Lord."

The Large and Small

They met on a green pathway in the woods. Who is more important? The small one or the large one? But who or what are we talking about? They are both God's creatures. The squirrel is representative of all the small creatures, whilst the horse is representative of the large creatures.

This meeting caused such a reaction from the squirrel that his whiskers quivered so fast they looked like windscreen washers on a car, caught in the rain. A horse can be spooked and rear up in fright. But this time his opponent was far too small. As the horse did not move, the squirrel looked up at him and said, "*What* are *you* doing here?"

The big horse perturbed said in reply, *"What* are *you* doing nearly under my feet?" With that, the squirrel shot up the nearest tree and the horse snorted – not that a beautifully trained horse, would do such a thing!

Imagine if a horse would snort loudly when in a special parade, he would not be popular with his rider at all. But man and horse can be bond well together in various situations. But I have not heard of man and squirrel bonding and forging a relationship. A squirrel can be trained to reach food, over obstacles, however. Squirrels live to roughly 15–18 years. They are small arboreal mammals that feed on seeds, nuts, berries and fungi. This is important for woodland eco-systems. They spread seeds of trees, and, also, spores of mycorrhizal fungi. Also like some birds, they can strip bark from trees to feed on the sap.

The seeds they scatter can lie dormant in the earth for many years. After many plus years these seeds can suddenly "pop up", after raging fires have burnt the earth. Slowly, a film of green will appear bringing *hope* for the future.

One of God's divine mysteries for nature to evolve.
We give Worship and Praise
To our Creative Father,
As we try to care for our ecosystems
And all nature in danger of being harmed
By the fast-changing climate temperatures.

The Frozen Lake

All around is quiet,
Still and motionless.
The invisible air
Seems motionless too.
The frozen lake
Reflects the sky.
No moving clouds
In fact, no clouds.
Can you hear or
Sense any living thing?
Slipping, sliding,
On a base not seeing
White or light.
A place non-existing,
Not conducting
Any life, or change,
Change or force,
Or life minute[1].

It takes –

A minuet[2] for music
in the air,
To take slipping, sliding
Dancers so fair.
To twirl in the air.
The air full of colours
That we see, in
Existing places; holding life
In the light and fluffy clouds.
The repeats and the wonder
Of six creation days.
Then the seventh revealing
Day, bringing rest and peace,
In our Frozen Lake, our World.
The world made by our Loving God
To care for,
With the use of free will.
But have we cared for
And maintained this precious gift
With all its creatures there-in?

- Minute – means extra tiny
- Minuet – a dance performed by couples, slowly and gracefully, supposedly, in past decades

Memory Time

(*With a special friend and all special friends over time.*)

Memory time is a precious time. We bring to mind those wonderful highlights of our time together. We worshipped in our home church, St Andrews of St Andrews – Scotland, you in your red choir robes and myself taking part and enjoying, the Episcopal Church service.

A venue we enjoyed specially was "The Cambo Estate", owned by the Erskine family for 300 years. Here we found snowdrops en masse or popping up in the most surprising places! You could also buy them in the green and have them mailed all over the UK. I sent some to North Wales and saw them blooming happily there the following year. A folktale called the snowdrops "little angels" because they were originally angels from the heavens, who had flown too near our earth, and their wings got caught in the mud forever. They had followed a human trait of being nosy!

Another aspect of visiting the Cambo Estate was their special gardens. They were kept beautifully. Vegetables growing amongst flowers and seed heads left to make interesting shapes; then they would be gathered in and sprayed with gold and silver to make Christmas decorations, for around the Big House. Together with holly and evergreen branches, these would also be sold at the usual Christmas Fair, to make money for the estate.

Once on another visit, we drove up a winding drive to find a *slow* sign in red. Underneath the warning were the words "*PIGLETS CROSSING*". Yes! Not deer crossing but "*PIGLETS CROSSING*". To add to the astonishment of us – they were an *orange* colour. Yes! *Orange*! We looked to the left and saw the piglets playing on the grass bank.

Looking right, we saw a hole in the fence, then the parental *large* pigs snuffling and grunting among large holly trees. But guess what? These huge pigs were *orange* too! It was plain to see beneath the mud on their large snouts (noses) as they searched for food. Then suddenly, with a rush, the orange piglets arrived to suckle form mum. It must have been lunchtime. It was certainly coffee tome for us, as we had laughed so much.

Note:- we have since learnt this breed of pig is called "The Tamworth Pig". They still compete in farming shows and often receive winning rosettes.

Before I draw to a close with this article, I will introduce you to another musical friend. She is a lovely lady who wore a splendid *blue* hat for my graduation. I wonder if she still has it! Anyway, she agreed to meet us at a place that was another favourite venue of ours, *"Kellie Castle"*. We had spent many happy visits there. Upon arrival, we were requested to meet up in the basement. The hour arrived and found us dutifully sitting around a *large* wooden table in the *large* kitchen. The truth was revealed – an afternoon tea had been arranged for us.

Several large cakes were set in front of us and a choice of teas to drink. The cakes were made from original Victorian recipes. A gigantic slice was lowered onto my plate. Now I am partial to eating cake – but – a cake made of seven layers with a different filling in each layer, defeated me!

Despite all this, our continuing friendship survives miles between us. God was with us, and still is.

Thank you Bodil, and
Thank you, Grace.
I send you both a Big Hug.

Girl in the Photograph

The girl in this photograph is not posing especially but trying to sell a hand-made article to a tourist. Artisans in this overseas country, in a co-operative setting, make beautiful woollen garments to sell to tourists. Smaller items can be made by the older children. Patterns and techniques are handed down through generations.

When all is ready for the tourist season, the children and some of the older girls are also prepared by dressing in their national costumes, full of colour. They are also adorned with shawls and brimmed hats. But one special preparation must not be missed. In different cultures, people think a pale or white complexion is much prettier than their own colouring. So, using a white powder – sometimes moist – the girls' faces are painted with it, as you can see in the photograph.

The photograph portrays such an expression of innocence on the young girl. But here, let us pause for a moment. Our society is both cruel and evil, good and bad. Evil can be spread like a spider's web. Thinking of situations that can arise these days or already actually happening, and as we read this article, one fears for the young girl and others like her. They could be drawn into the net of evil without realising what was or is happening.

Simply at first, certain people make friendly gestures and have conversations with the young people they have targeted for their purpose. The next step is grooming the susceptible young person. After a time, the chosen person only has thoughts to please their new friend. Eventually, the new "friend" is controlling the life of their victim who will do anything for them.

The aim to please is stronger than the request to carry out unlawful deeds for their friend. Slowly, these requests become threats, as the young person hesitates when the requests become more unlawful and dangerous. The situation and actions are now becoming criminal. The victim's innocence is slowly being replaced by fear. There becomes a penalty for not achieving what is asked of them. Quite often, violence becomes part of the situation for the groomed victim, as well as for others involved. These days school-aged children can, and do, become part of criminal plans and actions.

Realisation sets in as our first victim becomes aware of what life can really be like. I will not elaborate further, as to how the crime scenes ended up with so much evil in them. But many people ended up in very dark places. I will leave television, films and books to lay before you details of today's severe, problematic and grief-stricken situations. Very sadly, these occur all over the globe; with drugs and sex exploitation being two of the most horrific and life-changing outcomes. Stealing, lying and the aptitude towards violence becomes a normal way of life for the criminals who have no desire to change.

Many people are involved in trying to rescue victims from tense and dangerous situations. There are teams from police forces each highly trained; plus, international bodies that link up with other countries to follow the same trails of information until they reach a finite conclusion. Things are so much easier using modern technology these days, but human instinct and perception are still needed. There is a different body of people who are also very worried and concerned about the morality of not only this country, but every country as well as personal situations. We use, however, a different way of counteracting evil – *prayer*. Jesus of Nazareth picked His earthly disciples from fishermen and taught them to pray.

He also taught them to follow "His way". Now we, His modern disciples must aim to follow the same pathway and be strong enough to avoid temptation and evil. So that in time, we can leave a younger generation with an example to follow.

Ukraine

As I wrote about wars and terrorist activities in my first book, leading to Remembrance Day on 11 November, sadly now I write about Ukraine, and the Russian war – Russia being the aggressor and starting the war in 2022. The soldiers are violent and cruel in their fighting and seem to be working towards genocide, under orders, in their actions. There have been details recorded which show many war crimes have been committed in horrific circumstances.

Although the UK has been trying to help Ukraine in various ways e.g. volunteers taking to Ukraine in a convoy of vans, medicines, first Aid equipment, food and clothes, and offering homes to refugees who are fleeing their country. People are also without homes and have been reduced to living underground in cellars. Many have escaped with aid, especially children, but many of these have been targeted as the corridors of peace agreed by both sides, have been broken and fired upon. As I said in my previous book, you can access news reports daily from TV, radio and media sources.

Ukraine is an Orthodox Christian country, and where possible they hold funerals and prayers. But now the priests are having to go outside to pray for the mass graves that are being found; where innocent civilians, including children, lie. These are war crimes that point to the aggressor having thoughts of genocide as the soldiers attacking seem almost inhuman at times.

But one thing stands out at this time – the indomitable spirit and determination of the Ukraine army and the people staying in some small villages and blocks of flats in cities, refusing to leave their land and their homes. Villages and cities are rocketed into ruins, followed by marauding soldiers and Russian tanks. But the people left, stoutly go forth to rescue dead bodied and dig graves for them, wherever they can. They also try to apply First Aid to wounds for fighters, being older men or very young men who are learning how to *fight* and *defend* their country, as they go. Their defence is inspirational. They plan, fight and help each other, whilst masking their personal terror and fear.

Prayers and Love to Ukraine,
They already hold the cross of God.
He is with them in their suffering.

Empathy

Doing research for my donkey's, I find the character trait of empathy, showing up many times. I especially liked the story of a teenager who had been at the Manchester Bombing, but was able to walk away, but now has anxiety issues and flashbacks. She visited a donkey sanctuary and very much enjoyed meeting and talking to the animals and staff.

It was fortunate that her parents were able to give her a small piece of land where she started a small sanctuary for retired donkeys. On a TV interview, she told of the donkeys' empathy with her, which helped to relieve her flashbacks and anxiety issues. She said that when she sometimes wandered into the field holding the donkeys, and sat on a big stone seat, not feeling very good, as flashbacks to that so upsetting bombing in Manchester, came back, that she would find several donkeys wandering up to her and sit with her. She felt an unbelievable sense of empathy from them, and she felt comforted.

God not only gives human beings gifts to help each other, but to the animals to whom we can bond with; healing and supporting issues come God's grace.

The Question

Mermaids and mermen surface through time
From the watery caverns of the ocean deep.
Only to hear the same sounds of old,
Noise of warfare ceaselessly echoing
And reverberating across the oceanic valleys.

Not so different from the chaos
Caused by demonic sea monsters, who fought
To control God's creation, at the beginning of time.
That ideal world and peoples created by God,
Is being torn and ravaged by war and hate.
But continuing wars by women and men, are a human battle.
The power comes from the cosmic fight, between good and demonic evil.
Will it ever end in healing peace?

To sedately switch from past to present,
A new symbol emerges from the chrysalis stage.
It produces flowering force to counter evil –
Combining anima and animas of humans.
And here the mermaid and merman reappear in the form of Mer persons.
The force of equality in myth and legend
Making mermaid and merman into Mer person
Is an indication of how humanity is progressing
To make the past and the present as one.

Faith in Action

You walk up the mountain
To seek comfort from
Our Heavenly Father.
Open your arms in a plea
To find strength and motivation,
From your faith. I
Can feel God's love (unconditional)
Entering my heart and mind
When remembering the words of Jesus Christ-

*"Come to me, all who are weary and burdened,
and I will give you rest."*

We can experience the wilderness
And strength to go forward.
I am sad to see other people
Walking away from situations
That they feel irksome,
Or troublesome, to cope with.
We are not alone in this world.
Our Heavenly Father through
His Son Jesus Christ, is
Waiting to guide and help us, with love.

So be whom you are really are.
Believe in your faith and have confidence
And love, to go forward
With Christ. Remember always be
What you want to be and do.
Next time you open your arms,
May it be to someone who needs
Help and forgiveness. Using your
"Faith in Action", lead them to find
The path of Jesus Christ, and *His love.*

Autumn Meditation

How lovely to talk and meditate
With a fellow soul.
Sitting in a pretty garden,
Feeling the peace of God,
As we fell quiet at moments,
The rustle of the autumn
Leaves wraps around us
Like angels' wings.

We think of our dreams,
As they disappear up
Into the clouds, like
"The Lark Ascending" towards heaven.
A beautiful classical piece
Of music, by the composer
Ralph Vaughan Williams.
It is music dearly loved
By many people. It sets
Free many of our thoughts
And worries and problems,
So, we feel, like
"The Lark Ascending into
Heaven", into God's hands.

My friend and I sat
Gazing up at the clouds.
Do we see angels among
Drifting, or cumulus clouds?
Or our imaginative thoughts?
In this autumnal moment, we
Send our Love to Thee, Lord
And Worship, for our Creation.

Saint Augustine, one of the old Latin Fathers, has our respect from all his writings and teachings.

> *"The real world is spiritual, ours but a shadow."*
> St Augustine

Christmas and Later

A glimmer of Hope
A glimpse of Peace
Curiously waiting
For the night to appear,
When the babe of our hearts
Is here once again

We wait impatiently
For the dawning day
Where our Christ Child
Waits, at the edge
Of our hearts.
Behold – he knocks.

Let Him enter our lives,
Welcome Him with your love.
Follow Christ's pathway
And let Him lead us,
Onwards with courage
And resolution and joy.

Have You Lost Something?

Today, time are hard for many people. It is December and ten days from Christmas. It is usually an exciting time, especially for children, young and old!! The emphasis being on presents – gifts to family and friends, and as thank yous to people and organisations who have helped and cared for you through the past year.

District nurses

Carers

Cleaners

Neighbourhood groups who offer snacks and companionship

Volunteers and neighbours who do shopping and errands for you especially if you live alone.

I'm sure you could make a list of your own. Do not forget grannies and grandads, or whatever your children call them – the good fairies when times get tough! *So for you, yourself,* I've written the following words, seriously!

The Jewel of Christmas

What are jewels? The shiniest things that flash in the light, the faceted cut of pieces of rock – or the safe arrival of a new-born baby? These are things that can be found or happen, at any time of year. But why do they carry such emphasis at Christmas time? Shall we explore the point and find answers, although they may not be acceptable to all of us? We have differing opinions between many of us. These can be a result of so many changes in our lives, driven by age, culture, chronic health conditions and financial situations. Our thoughts can be reshaped, and personalities changed maybe, as we experience life in all its differing guises.

Can the death of a beloved one lead us to looking forward to the birth of a new baby? Does this bring us the *anticipation* of a new happiness to come, the filling of an empty shape in our lives? New promise awaits us – new love to come. But how that love will change humanity, from its birth, growing stronger and more fulfilling as time passes?

So we wait in *anticipation* for that feeling, on Christmas morning. It is here again once more, that wondrous gift has arrived for every one of us.

"The Holy Babe of Bethlehem"
bringing God's Unconditional Love.

Angel of Hope

    An Angel of Hope spends a lot of time on Earth as her wings – especially the bottom ones – are suggestive of autumn leaves packed closely together giving them a lovely golden – brown hue. The top half of her wings are luxuriant and point upwards towards the sky emphasising her heavenly connection. The top half of her wings are also like flames and again this could emphasise her connection to Earth with another Earth element – of fire. She is a very approachable figure suggested by her arms which appear to be outstretched as if she is beckoning to the viewer to come to her and she will offer help.

The Nativity

In this last section of my book, we encounter the changing weather temperatures of winter. But we also receive anew the most wonderous gift we will ever receive, experience. This is given to us from our Father, God Almighty, through his grace and love.

I start this "nativity story", from the very beginning.

Mary, a young maiden, was going about her chores when suddenly the Archangel Gabriel appeared to her. She remained calm but stunned and utterly astonished. The angel spoke to her. Here we pause for the question – what are angels? The simplest answer for the moment is *winged messengers from God*, and it is believed by many that they were created by God, on the second day of his creation of the earth.

The angels in the first instance, act as a bridge between heaven and Earth. This becomes a channel between God and our physical world, which carries the divine love – and message for us (humanity). The word angel is derived from the Greek work *angelos*, meaning angel.

Note – if you are interested in learning about Angel-Lore, there are many books available and on the internet. The topic comes under Angelology *and the Bible mentions angels throughout history.*

The Archangel Gabriel is the ruler of heaven, the first one from our earth. It is thought to be paradise where Adam and Eve first dwell before they were sent out by God. This heaven can be known as the Garden of Eden, where Eve and then Adam ate of the fruit of the Tree of Life. To do this had been forbidden by God. But they had disobeyed this rule. *(Refer back to the beginning of the book – Spring, Easter Passion.)*

This garden is where the Tree of Life and Knowledge grows. This first heaven is called Vilon, and it is derived from the Latin word *Velum,* which means *veil.* Sometimes, you hear the belief that this first heaven is the nearest one to our earth over the veil separating us. In total, there are seven heavens. These are the

Spiritual Realms. Various Archangels rule over these heavens. The seventh heaven is where God is known to be.

I continue with the appearance of the Archangel Gabriel to Mary. We call it *"The immaculate Conception"*.

In talking about Mary, we find the words – lowly maiden – applied to her. This shows how far down Mary is placed in the hierarchy of the culture in those days. God had chosen not a rich and ruling family, a powerful one, but a family that was poor and unimportant in status. But the lowly maiden that was chosen, Mary, was good in character and followed the scriptures earnestly. She was betrothed to Joseph, a carpenter from the house of David – a royal line. In those times, everyone followed, and were very aware of, their family line (genealogy). Today not many people do. Sometimes a family member will be exceptionally interested and have a family tree drawn up for them to regularly follow and keep up to date.

We realise from the scriptures, how God's thoughts and ways differ from ours. We might ask a question of him and expect to receive an answer straight away almost. But *God will answer in his own time.* But how does God's time work? Who knows? For example, would you have your baby, or any baby, arrive in a stable full of differing cattle in the middle of winter? But there again we do have babies arriving in str age places even in these days! Also, another example, do we see a host of angels, singing in the night sky, whenever a baby is born here and now. Mind you, someone might, after having one (or maybe two) drinks to celebrate the baby's birth – to wet the baby's head as it can be called. In some cases, according to cultural or religious faiths, a small party with emphasis on food, would take place.

The angel Gabriel, sent by God, appeared to Mary and said, 'Greetings, favoured one! The Lord is with you.' (Luke 1: 12 NRSV) Mary was puzzled, astonished and stunned. But seeing this, Gabriel told her not to be afraid, because the Lord was with her. She would conceive in her womb and have a Son whom she would call Jesus. Mary replied to the angel Gabriel, again very puzzled, that how could this happen as she had not been with a man. The Archangel said to her in reply, 'The Holy Spirit will come upon you, and the power of the Most High will overshadow you. Therefore, the child to be born will be holy; he will be called Son of God. And now you relative, Elizabeth, has also conceived a son, in her old age. She is now six months into her pregnancy.' She was always referred as barren, but nothing is impossible for God.

After hearing Gabriel's news, Mary then said, 'Here am I, the servant of the Lord, let it be with me according to your word.' Then the Archangel Gabriel left her. Mary then remembered something the angel had said to her – that the Lord God would give to her Son, the throne of the ancestor, David, where he would reign over the house of Jacob forever – reference back to the writing of genealogy, and how important it was to the people of that age. Also noted down in the Old Testament of the Bible.

Note: Here we have used text from St Luke's gospel. He is known as having written his gospel for the gentiles and unlike St Matthew's gospel, where it is known as written for the Jews.

Zechariah and the Meeting of the Two Cousins

After the message from the Archangel Gabriel, Mary went quickly to see her cousin, Elizabeth.

She and her husband, Zechariah, lived in a Judean town, in the hill country. He belonged to the priestly order of Abijah, and his wife was a descendant of Aaron. Although both of them had lived blameless and righteous lives before God, Elizabeth was barren, but was quite old. Now Zechariah was on duty at the temple, and it was his turn to enter the sanctuary (or Holy of Holies) to offer incense to the Lord. A whole assembly of people were praying outside.

As Zechariah went in, he saw the angel by the altar and was terrified. But the angel Gabriel told him not to be afraid. Then he said to him that his prayers to God had been heard. For Zechariah and Elizabeth had prayed earnestly to the Lord for a child, practically all their married life. Then Gabriel continued with the news from God, that Elizabeth would have a child and they would name him *John.* He would bring joy and gladness and be great in the sight of God. But, Gabriel admonished, John must never drink strong drink; even before his birth, he will possess the Holy Spirit. He will turn many of Israel's people to the Lord. With the Holy Spirit and the power of Elijah, he would turn parents' hearts to their children, and the disobedient to the wisdom of God-fearing people who had faith and trusted their Lord God. With these changes, there then would be a people ready and prepared for the Lord – the coming Messiah.

Reference: Luke 1: 10–17

John, as we now know, is John, the Baptist.

After listening to the Angel Gabriel, Zechariah was doubtful about the message and queries it, saying that both he and his wife were too old. The angel replied that he had been sent by God to bring him this happy message. But since Zechariah had doubted the angel and therefore God, he would be mute until the baby was born – mute meaning unable to speak. So as Gabriel departed, Zechariah left the sanctuary and faced the people outside. They had been waiting for so long and when the priest kept motioning to them, but obviously could not speak, they realised he must have, perhaps, seen a vision. So after his service at the temple finished, Zechariah just went quietly home.

After several months, when his wife was carrying a child, Zechariah knew he had been wrong in doubting the angel, Gabriel. After six months he was further amazed by a visit from Elizabeth's cousin, Mary. She brought further news for them.

Upon reaching their house, Mary and Elizabeth clasped hands tightly. They felt a special connection and Elizabeth put her arm around Mary's shoulders and proclaimed, after hearing Mary's words, that the child in her womb had "leapt for joy". (Luke 1: 41–42)

Elizabeth was filled with the Holy Spirit. She added in astonishment that Mary was *blessed* and also, she, herself – because the mother of her Lord had visited her with this news. Then Mary herself said, 'My Soul magnifies the Lord, and my spirit rejoices in God – My Saviour.' Then Mary continued with her Song of Praise.

This song we now know as *The Magnificat.* This is sung all over the world in very many churches, cathedrals, and monasteries. You can also find it printed in books and musical scores and on audio CDs. The art-work that accompanies some of these books and musical scores is fantastic. You can learn so much from reading them especially the Magnificat.

- *Note: Elizabeth and Zechariah live in the Judean hills and this place is known as "celebration". An old translation of the Hebrew place name.*
- *This is where the world first celebrates the Incarnation of the Son of God.*
- *The biblical text of the Magnificat is found in the gospel of St Luke. Luke 1: 46–55*

Mary stayed for about three months with Elizabeth, then journeyed home.

John the Baptist

The cousin of Mary, Elizabeth, when her time was due, gave birth to a baby boy. As was instructed by Gabriel, the Arch Angel, the baby was named John. He grew up strong and was filled with the Holy Spirit.

John was known as "The Prophet from the Desert". He ate the simplest of food. I am sure that many of you have heard of locusts that flourish in the desert. Some people today eat them and remark that although they are insects, they can be quite tasty and crunchy. According to the law of Moses – certain kinds of locusts are considered as "clean food". Perhaps you might think that wild honey, as John ate in the desert, could be a preferable food. There are certain trees also in the desert, that are known under the *akrides.*

They are trees that grow pods. The pods look mottled like locusts, and form together in close knit bunches. These trees are called carob trees, or locust bean trees. This is the translation from *akrides*, from the original term for these trees from the Greek. Carob seeds (beans) were found from 6000BC. As John ate these, they became known as "St John's Bread". They are naturally sweet and contain vitamins and minerals. Wild honey was also found in the desert and herbs and medicinal roots and leaves.

After many years, John began to preach about the coming Messiah. He gathered a number of disciples around him. Some people asked if he was the Messiah. To which John replied,

'I baptise you with water, but the one who is more powerful than I is coming; I am not worthy to untie his sandals. He will baptise you with the Holy Spirit and with fire.' (Luke 3: 16)

Then John carried on with his teaching at Bethany.

A few days later, john saw his cousin Jesus walking towards him. Jesus asked John to baptise him. He was a little reluctant at first, but Jesus replied that this must be adhered to as their religion so instructed (for the moment.) So John baptised Jesus in the River Jordan. As Jesus rose from the water, the heavens opened and a dove flew down and landed on him. Then a loud voice was heard saying, 'This is my beloved son in whom I am well pleased.' The dove represented the Holy Spirit.

After the baptism, John went on his way with his disciples, teaching and foretelling of the Messiah that was now with them. He made a strange remark in his teaching. 'Now,' he said to his disciples, 'as the Messiah has come, I must decrease as he increases.' Sadly, this ended very abruptly for John. He was thrown into prison, then after a while he was decapitated. The story is told in detail in the Gospel of Matthew. (Matt 14: 1–12) Hearing the news of his death, Jesus, his cousin and Messiah, was very sad. The two cousins first met in their mothers' wombs when Mary and Elizabeth met to reveal God's messages to them. Elizabeth said that when she heard Mary's message from God, the baby, John in her womb, jumped for joy. This is the real visitation between Mary and Elizabeth, of course, the real encounter, between John the Baptist and Jesus.

There are two points to think about here, firstly Mary with the baby Jesus. Mary now represents the future and more openness to God. She is now a "God-bearer" (*Theotokos*). Secondly, Elizabeth gives birth to John the Baptist, who is the last of the prophets. This shows the future with a different emphasis on worship and our understanding of the new covenant with God, that Jesus spoke to us from the Cross.

Mary and Joseph

After Mary received the message from the Arch Angel Gabriel, she went straightaway to visit her cousin, Elizabeth. Perhaps she wondered what her betrothed future husband, Joseph, was feeling or would feel, when she arrived home after staying with Elizabeth for three months; for she was obviously pregnant by then. Or did she think, with her faith so strong, that her Lord would have prepared Joseph for the wonder of the situation.

Matt 1: 18–25

Joseph being a righteous man had planned to dismiss Mary quietly, to avoid all the shame and disgrace she would have received, for being pregnant before their marriage. But then an angel appeared to Joseph in his sleep. In the dream, the angel said to him that he should not be afraid to take Mary as his wife, for the child she was carrying was from the Holy Spirit (i.e., God). The angel also told Joseph that Mary would give birth to a son, and he should name him Jesus. This child would come to save his people from their king. We now know this child, the Messiah, would lead his people to a new creation and a new covenant with God.
(Refer back to the Easter Passion at the beginning of this book to know how this would occur.)

When he awoke, Joseph did as the angel said. He took Mary for his wife. However, he had no marital relations with her until she had her first-born son and named him Jesus.

Mary and Joseph Journey to Bethlehem

Luke 2: 1–7
Luke 2: 16–19

A first registration while Quirinius was governor of Syria was ordered. A decree went out from the Emperor Augustus that everyone should be registered. To do this everyone had to go to their own towns. Joseph, taking Mary, travelled from Nazareth in Galilee to Judea, to the city David called Bethlehem. Joseph was descended from the house and family of David. He also took Mary to whom he was engaged. She was with child. They searched and searched for a lodging, but everywhere was full. Finally, an innkeeper who was sympathetic towards them – Mary looked so tired and was heavily pregnant – that he offered them the use of his stable, although it had cattle in it.

- *Mary and Joseph accepted the innkeeper's offer. At least they could take their tired donkey with them. He had carried Mary all the way from Nazareth.*
- *Towards the end of his life, Jesus also rode on a young donkey. He asked his disciples to bring him one so he could ride into Jerusalem. We now call that day* Palm Sunday.

At the Stable

In the stable, Mary gave birth to her first son. The stable was not the clean and comfortable place that one sees in pictures, or Christmas plays that are performed each year by children in schools or churches. The stable was cold and dirty, full of cobwebs and very smelly. In one book, I read it was suggested that perhaps Joseph himself swept out the floor and the old manure, then relaced with dry straw and a clean robe for Mary. This was the place where the encounter between God and Humankind took place.

It was not very an impressive building with royal drapes hung on the walls, and attendees all around, as in King Hero's palace. But it was there in that stable shared with a bullock and cattle, and a precious little donkey. Overhead were angels singing.

The Birth, The Door of Faith, Split

Part of the "Door of Faith" that hangs in the Cathedral of St Dominus in Split, in Croatia has an image of the Nativity. It was carved by the great and excellent master *Andrija* in the year 1214. Why precisely this door? I am writing these verses from the book I have been using – "The Door of Split" 2014. If you can see if you can find it online. For this illustration, words from the Gospel Luke 2: 1–7 were used. Most of my Gospel references in this section have been from St Luke's Gospel.

One enters and comes through the door,
Goes into the world and returns home!
These are the doors that echo:
Open the door to Christ!
These are the doors of faith.
These are the doors to life.
These doors,

In 28 evangelical images,

Are inviting us:
Enter the gates of the Lord with thanksgiving
And his courts with praise!

God wished for the world's animals to be part of his creation under humankind's care. Most importantly, in that stable, were loving hearts and souls. Legend says that a little bird flapped its wings – so hard – to keep the little fire going, to give out warmth for the tiny baby. The little bird scorched its chest. Now that bird is known as Robin Redbreast.

News for the Shepherds

It was a cold, still night. Some shepherds were huddled in their bits of cloaks round a tiny fire. The sheep seemed still. A few stars just lay in the sky. *Suddenly,* all around was lit by a wondrous light and the sky twinkled with a myriad of stars. Warmth encompassed the shepherds and looking upwards they saw an angel form the heavens – the Archangel Gabriel. They heard the angel speak to them.

"Fear not, for behold I bring you great tidings which will be for all men. For unto you is born this day, in the city of David (Bethlehem), a Saviour who us Christ the Lord. You shall see this babe lying in a manger."

Luke 1: 8–11

And suddenly there was with the angel a heavenly host praising God and saying,
'Glory to God in the highest and on earth Peace and Goodwill to all men.'

After the angels had gone away, the shepherds discussed what they had seen and heard. Then one of them said, perhaps they should go and see this baby which the angels had told them about. So as all the shepherds agreed, they formed a group not forgetting the young shepherd boy to whom they gave a tiny new-born lamb to carry. This was to be a present for the baby Jesus. Then they started on their journey –following a bright star, which seemed to go before them.

Note: a collapsed star gravitates towards a black hole. Then slowly drifts into our galactic core.

The date of Christ's human birth was approximately 2023 years ago. This leads us to think of earlier information of stars in God's creation. The myriad stars the shepherds saw was in existence in our Milky-Way and galaxy long before that time. The original formation of our Milky-Way was infiltrated by the "Sagittarius A Star" way, way back in our galaxy's history. Our intelligence and gathered learning from all sections of science lead us back further through billions of non-imaginable time scales. Now through scientific discoveries and deductions they begin to glimpse our astronomic future. (To some critics – maybe!)

The famous "Sagittarius A Star" ends up in a black hole, one amongst others. To find out what happened to that particular black hole, follow the new book and series on "Exploring the Universe". (Foreword by Prof. Brian Cox.) Intriguingly we need to read the late Stephen Hawking's paper on "Black Holes". Here he refutes the notion that nothing can escape from black holes. "Black holes are not tombs *– but live on!" He decrees.*

This note about stars leads us back to the shepherds' view of the myriad stars accompanying the angels, singing in praise of God. This was after the Archangel Gabriel announced the news of the birth of baby Jesus, in the stable in Bethlehem.

Once again, God has chosen to bring wonderful news to the *lowly* of that time and culture. How did the shepherds react? They immediately went to Bethlehem, following the star as their guide, to see the baby Messiah. When Gabriel announced God's message to Mary she responded in the affirmative without hesitation. Her love and duty for God was the uppermost thought in her mind. She was to receive verbal insults and scathing remarks from people who realised she was pregnant before her marriage to Joseph. Was she hurt by this, or were her feelings solely for the protection of her unborn child – *the wondrous gift from God – the gift to the world?*

I wonder if the young shepherd lad always remembered that night.

Did it alter his life perhaps, or did he even see Jesus when Jesus was preaching during his ministry?

Sadly, did the young shepherd lad hear, or see, the crucifixion of Jesus – that tiny babe born in a stable?

When the young lad reached manhood, how did his life progress?

Perhaps that is another story!

Final Thoughts

I hope I have extended just a little your knowledge and faith of God and his love for us. May we listen for God's Holy Spirit and to lead us, as we pray with love to God, through Jesus Christ his son.

I have no answers here for you. Your own answers must come from communion between you and God. May I ask you – what do you want from your Christian faith? Maybe a way of life you think is good and proper and can be seen as you attend church and stand proud? Or maybe you want to have a steadfast shelter under God's wing, as you have to cope with earthly trials and tribulations – a phrase we all recognise. But what would you do to thank God. God has his own way of meeting you. I wish you well in any spiritual journey you may wish to follow, to learn further knowledge and deeper faith.

> Lord, abide with us.
> May you find inner peace.

Jesus Christ brought heaven down to us, as he suffered on the cross. There he worked to save God's creation and bring forgiveness to all. As we reach out to God in despair, Christ brings us hope and Love from his Father God. As we struggle to find our lost way through troubled times, the light of Christ will shine before us, and lead onwards to a pathway of strength and purpose.

"How great thou art", a phrase from the hymn, encapsulates the joy we feel as we worship together and receive God's grace, into our lives.

I could not end this book without writing a tribute to Queen Elizabeth II. Like so many people, I heard the announcement of her death yesterday afternoon 8 September 2022, with great sadness.

I also saw the *rainbow* that appeared over Buckingham Palace in the early evening. This was so significant to me personally. A *rainbow* carried the message of God's new covenant to us, all those years ago.

I use a piece here I wrote and have used ever since. With a heartfelt "Thank you" to our beloved Queen Elizabeth II, I invite you to read, and think of the "The Circle of Love".

Irene Smith

From Belief Beyond Pain by Jenny Francis 1992
"White light is made up of colours of the spectrum. There would not be that transparent purity if there were no dark indigo included. And the rainbow shows that each shade is a sign of God's covenant."

The Circle of Love

It is not time to say goodbye, for our souls live on forever. They carry the love they found on earth into eternity, and link into the Circle of Love that encompasses humanity on earth and leads into timeless eternity.

It is but a short time we spend on earth, taking part in God's creation. We find our own aspects of beauty and use God-given talents to maintain and record that beauty as.

(Name of deceased and place in family)

We cherish the memories of people we have loved; and these memories join our Circle of Love.

Negative thoughts and negative remembrances from us – fade into nothingness and exist no more. Fond and happy memories live on with us, bringing tranquillity and peace for us to accept, in our own time.

The Circle of Love welcomes home every soul, released from suffering and the trials on earth. Think of .... resting in eternal peace, love and joy.

Eternity Is Timeless

Love is Eternity Love is the Way
The Circle of life and Love

Past – Present – and Future
There is never any conclusion.
The conclusion of Life and Love
Goes on turning and turning.
It takes us to Eternity,
We become part of Infinity.

Infinity becomes for us
The tiniest dot seen by
The naked eye, upon the
Horizon, the tiniest, tiniest
Pinprick of light, seen through
Technology's newest aid,
Helps us to see into the
Beyond – and more.

Our thoughts when we see
Into the unknown, leave the
Technological plane behind.
Then centre a swirling
Mass of undefined emotion.

Has Science been replaced
By Religion? Or has Religion
Been replaced by Science?
Maybe the two go
Hand in hand, or just exist
On a human level.
Perhaps the swirling mass
Of emotion, is left undefined.

Bibliography

NSRV Bible
The Doors of Faith, Split Cathedral
Publisher: Museum for Sacral Arts – Split
The Universe Andrew Cohen.
Foreword: Brian Cox
Publisher: William Collins
ISBN: 0008389322